Greetings from
GEORGIA

Greetings from
GEORGIA

Greetings from
GEORGIA

Greetings from
GEORGIA

Greetings from
GEORGIA

Greetings from
GEORGIA

Greetings from
GEORGIA

Greetings from
GEORGIA

Greetings from
GEORGIA

Greetings from
GEORGIA

Greetings from
GEORGIA

Greetings from
GEORGIA

Greetings from
GEORGIA

Greetings from
GEORGIA

Greetings from
GEORGIA

Greetings from
GEORGIA

Greetings from
GEORGIA

Greetings from
GEORGIA

Greetings from
GEORGIA

Greetings from
GEORGIA

Greetings from
GEORGIA

Greetings from
GEORGIA

Greetings from
GEORGIA

Greetings from
GEORGIA

Greetings from
GEORGIA

Greetings from
GEORGIA

Greetings from
GEORGIA

Greetings from
GEORGIA

Greetings from
GEORGIA

Greetings from
GEORGIA

Greetings from
GEORGIA

Greetings from
GEORGIA

Greetings from
GEORGIA

Greetings from
GEORGIA

Greetings from
GEORGIA

Greetings from
GEORGIA

Greetings from
GEORGIA

Greetings from
GEORGIA

Greetings from
GEORGIA

Greetings from
GEORGIA

Greetings from
GEORGIA

Greetings from
GEORGIA

Greetings from
GEORGIA

Greetings from
GEORGIA

Greetings from
GEORGIA

Greetings from
GEORGIA

Greetings from
GEORGIA

Greetings from
GEORGIA

Greetings from
GEORGIA

Greetings from
GEORGIA

Greetings from
GEORGIA

Greetings from
GEORGIA

Greetings from
GEORGIA

Greetings from
GEORGIA

Greetings from
GEORGIA

Greetings from
GEORGIA

Greetings from
GEORGIA

Greetings from
GEORGIA

Greetings from
GEORGIA

Greetings from
GEORGIA

Greetings from
GEORGIA

Greetings from
GEORGIA

Greetings from
GEORGIA

Greetings from
GEORGIA

Greetings from
GEORGIA

Greetings from
GEORGIA

Greetings from
GEORGIA

Greetings from
GEORGIA

Greetings from
GEORGIA

Greetings from
GEORGIA

Greetings from
GEORGIA

Greetings from
GEORGIA

Greetings from
GEORGIA

Greetings from
GEORGIA

Greetings from
GEORGIA

Printed in the USA
CPSIA information can be obtained
at www.ICGtesting.com
CBHW020833260624
10675CB00006B/752

9 798385 41167